EXTREME DINOSAURS

WORLD'S SCARIEST DINOSAURS

Rupert Matthews

Heinemann Library
Chicago, Illinois

www.capstonepub.com
Visit our website to find out more information about Heinemann-Raintree books.

To order:
☏ Phone 800-747-4992
▭ Visit www.capstonepub.com to browse our catalog and order online.

Edited by Rebecca Rissman and Laura Knowles
Designed by Richard Parker
Picture research by Mica Brancic
Originated by Capstone Global Library Ltd
Printed and bound in the United States of America
in North Mankato, Minnesota.   102012   007000RP

15 14 13 12
10 9 8 7 6 5 4 3 2

Library of Congress Cataloging-in-Publication Data
Matthews, Rupert.
  World's scariest dinosaurs / Rupert Matthews.
      p. cm.—(Extreme dinosaurs)
  Includes bibliographical references and index.
  ISBN 978-1-4109-4525-9 (hb)—ISBN 978-1-4109-4532-7
(pb) 1. Dinosaurs—Juvenile literature. I. Title.
  QE861.5.M3746 2012
  567.912—dc23   2011016096

Acknowledgments
We would like to thank the following for permission to reproduce images: © Capstone Publishers pp. **4** (James Field), **5** (James Field), **6** (James Field), **7** (Steve Weston), **8** (James Field), **9** (James Field), **10** (Steve Weston), **11** (Steve Weston), **12** (Steve Weston), **13** (James Field), **14** (James Field), **15** (Steve Weston), **16** (James Field), **17** (James Field), **18** (James Field), **19** (James Field), **20** (James Field), **21** (James Field), **23** (Steve Weston), **25** (Steve Weston); © Miles Kelly Publishing pp. **24** (Fiametta Dogi), **27** (Mike Saunders); iStockphoto p. **29** (© Arpad Benedek).

Background design features reproduced with permission of Shutterstock/© Szefei/© Fedorov Oleksiy/© Oleg Golovnev/© Nuttakit.

Cover image of a *Tyrannosaurus* reproduced with permission of © Capstone Publishers/James Field.

We would like to thank Nathan Smith for his invaluable help in the preparation of this book.

Every effort has been made to contact copyright holders of material reproduced in this book. Any omissions will be rectified in subsequent printings if notice is given to the publisher.

Disclaimer
All the Internet addresses (URLs) given in this book were valid at the time of going to press. However, due to the dynamic nature of the Internet, some addresses may have changed, or sites may have changed or ceased to exist since publication. While the author and publisher regret any inconvenience this may cause readers, no responsibility for any such changes can be accepted by either the author or the publisher.

Contents

Some words are shown in bold, **like this**.
You can find out what they mean by
looking in the glossary.

A Scary World

The world was a terrifying place 100 million years ago. **Dinosaurs** far larger than any animal alive today walked the land. Some of them were fierce hunters, while others were scary beasts with horns and spikes.

The Tyrant King

Tyrannosaurus was a huge meat eater that lived in North America. It could open its strong jaws very wide, ready to plunge its teeth into **prey**. *Tyrannosaurus* did not only hunt for live food. It used its sense of smell to find dead, rotting bodies that it could feast on.

Tyrannosaurus

Did You Know?

Tyrannosaurus's sharp teeth were almost 10 inches long. That's longer than your lower arm!

Fatty Terror

Spinosaurus may have been the most massive hunting **dinosaur** of them all. It weighed about 20 tons. That is the same as four Asian elephants! *Spinosaurus* probably hunted large fish in rivers or swamps. The hump on its back may have been made of fat, similar to a camel's hump. This fat would have been used when food was hard to find.

Did You Know?

Some scientists think *Spinosaurus* may also have hunted other dinosaurs.

9

Clawed Killer

Deinonychus was a lethal killing machine. It hunted in groups known as packs. This meant it could kill and eat animals much larger than itself. *Deinonychus* could run almost 30 miles per hour when hunting— that is as fast as a race horse!

Did You Know?

Deinonychus had a curved claw on its back leg that was 5 inches long. It probably used this to slash at victims.

Deinonychus

Handy Hunter

The meat eater *Acrocanthosaurus* measured almost 30 feet long. That is as long as two cars. It caught **prey** using its front legs. These were very strong. The clawed fingers could bend forward or backward easily.

Did You Know?

Acrocanthosaurus probably grabbed a victim with its clawed arms so tightly that it could not escape. The prey was then bitten to death and gobbled up.

Spiked Lizard

Styracosaurus had so many spikes on its head that it was given a name that means "spiked lizard." The spikes grew from the back of its skull and were very sharp. Perhaps they were weapons to fight off hunters. This **dinosaur** was about 18 feet long, which is three times longer than a motorcycle.

Mystery Killer

Baryonyx was about 28 feet long, which is as long as five sofas pushed end to end. It is a mystery how it found its food. Some scientists think it used its long, sharp claws to kill other **dinosaurs** for food. Others believe it used its small, sharp teeth to catch fish in rivers. Nobody really knows.

Did You Know?

Scientists named the animal *Baryonyx walkeri* after William Walker, who found the **fossils** when out for a walk.

Crested Hunter

Dilophosaurus was a hunter that had two crests on its head. Its teeth pointed backward and its jaw had a kink in it. These may have helped *Dilophosaurus* catch small **prey** such as fish. The first *Dilophosaurus* **fossil** to be found had no crest, so the scientist who discovered it left it off his drawing of the **dinosaur**.

Did You Know?
In the film *Jurassic* Park, *Dilophosaurus* is shown with a neck frill. No such frill existed.

19

Tyrant Ancestor

The hunting **dinosaur** *Guanlong* lived in China. It was almost 10 feet long. It could run quickly, leaping to pounce on **prey** and tear them to pieces. It may have lived on the shores of lakes and on riverbanks. It is thought that *Guanlong* was related to *Tyrannosaurus*.

Guanlong

Twilight Hunter

Twilight was no time to relax. The hunter *Stenonychosaurus* had very large eyes so it could see well at night. It would **stalk** and kill when others were sleeping.

Stenonychosaurus may have had feathers on its head and arms. These were probably brightly colored and were held upright to scare away other dinosaurs.

feathers

23

Thick Heads

One group of plant-eating **dinosaurs** had very thick skulls made of almost solid bone. They are known as Pachycephalosaurs, which means "thick-headed lizards." *Wannanosaurus* was one of the earliest of these dinosaurs. It was about 3 feet long. *Pachycephalosaurus* was the biggest. It was as long as a large car. Perhaps the dinosaurs head-butted each other in fights.

Wannanosaurus

Pachycephalosaurus

bony skull

Did You Know?
The skull of *Pachycephalosaurus* was almost 8 inches thick.

Elasmosaurus

Dinosaurs were not the only giant creatures to live during the **Mesozoic Era**. Gigantic **reptiles** lived in the sea. Turtles grew to be over 13 feet across— as big as a backyard swimming pool. Ichthyosaurs were reptiles that looked and behaved like dolphins. Plesiosaurs were reptiles with large bodies and long necks.

Elasmosaurus

How to Become a Paleontologist

Scientists who study **dinosaurs** and other **ancient** animals are called paleontologists. After finishing school, students study at college to learn how to become a paleontologist. They learn how to find **fossils** and how to study them. Paleontologists need to know about the many different kinds of ancient life. It is possible to be a part-time paleontologist. Some people look for fossils as a hobby on weekends and on vacations and holidays.

29

Glossary

ancient describes something that lived a very long time ago

dinosaur group of animals that lived on land millions of years ago during the Mesozoic Era

fossil part of a plant or animal that has been buried in rocks for millions of years

Jurassic part of Earth's history that began about 200 million years ago and ended about 145 million years ago

Mesozoic Era part of Earth's history that is sometimes called the "Age of Dinosaurs." It is divided into three periods: Triassic, Jurassic, and Cretaceous.

prey animal that is killed by another for food

reptiles cold-blooded animals such as lizards or crocodiles

rival dinosaur competing with another for something such as food

stalk follow quietly and carefully so as not to be heard or seen

twilight time in the evening when the Sun is setting but it is not yet dark

Find Out More

Books

Bingham, Caroline. *Dinosaur Encyclopedia.* New York: Dorling Kindersley, 2009.

Lessem, Don. *The Ultimate Dinopedia.* Washington, DC: National Geographic Children's Books, 2010.

Markarian, Margie. *Who Cleans Dinosaur Bones?* Chicago: Heinemann-Raintree, 2010.

Matthews, Rupert. *Ripley Twists: Dinosaurs.* Orlando, FL: Ripley Publishing, 2010.

Websites

science.nationalgeographic.com/science/prehistoric-world.html
Learn more about dinosaurs and other facts about the prehistoric world at this National Geographic Website.

www.ucmp.berkeley.edu/
Learn more about fossils, prehistoric times, and paleontology at this Website of the University of California Museum of Paleontology.

www.nhm.ac.uk/kids-only/dinosaurs
The Natural History Museum is located in London, England. Its Website has a lot of information about dinosaurs, including facts, quizzes, and games.

www.kidsdinos.com/
Play dinosaur games and read about dinosaurs on this Website.

Index